The Small Business Owner's Tax Guide

What every small business owner must know about reducing taxes

by Katryna Johnson, J.D.

COPYRIGHT (c) 2007, 2012 by KLJ Ventures, LLC

ALL RIGHTS RESERVED

Produced in the United States of America

Library of Congress Cataloging in Publication Data:

Author Katryna Johnson

Small Business Owner's Tax Guide

ISBN: 978-1479116256

Table of Contents

WHY I WROTE THIS BOOK

A middle-aged couple was sitting in my law office, intending to file bankruptcy. They had been trying so hard to make their home improvement company a success. But they had borrowed against their home, they had used up their savings, they had ruined their personal credit.

They were at the end of their financial rope. The stress and anxiety had finally gotten to be too much. The wife had been working a fairly low-wage job just to keep a roof over their head. But they had fallen behind, and now the mortgage company was filing foreclosure.

I was going through my standard bankruptcy interview. We talked about the business and what kinds of jobs he had done and what was in the pipeline. I asked to see their last three years of tax returns. He had done them himself using an online service.

I knew immediately that we had discovered a problem. He had included his wife's W-2, and all of his business income. He had taken the mortgage interest deduction, and some charity donations.

They had owed approximately $700 one year, $2,500 in year two, and $2,000 in year three. They had managed to pay these tax bills (they firmly believed in fulfilling their obligations – the thought of bankruptcy was killing them emotionally). Where were the business deductions? Where was Schedule C? His answer: he didn't know what he could take, it was too hard to keep track of things like mileage, and it wouldn't be that much, anyway.

Boy, was he wrong. Long story short: we re-figured his taxes for the past three years, taking every deduction we could legitimately recreate from his records and ended up getting almost $4,000 back from the IRS.

I then started a quest to educate small business owners about taxes. The result is this book. The tax law is complicated, and I don't claim to have all the answers. The content contained herein is not intended to substitute for legal, financial planning, investment or accounting service that is specific to you.

You need to review your finances with licensed professionals in those areas. I have to specifically disclaim all liability, loss or risk, personal or otherwise, incurred as a consequence directly or indirectly of the use or application of any of the techniques or contents in this book.

My hope is that this information helps you run a more successful small business. It is not intended to be a complete review of the entire tax code, rather it should alert you to areas you may need to research further and discuss with your accountant, bookkeeper, tax professional and business attorney.

INTRODUCTION

TAXES, taxes, taxes. You shouldn't run a small business without understanding at least a little about tax deductions. They are a fact of life, especially a business life. Thousands, if not millions, of small business owners overpay taxes each and every year because they are not educated on all of the possible allowable tax deductions they can take.

And it's no wonder. The tax code is complicated. In law school, I had to take two semesters on tax law, and we only scratched the surface.

But the complication of the tax code should be no excuse for educating yourself. The fact is: no one should overpay taxes -- ever. The tax laws are meant to be followed, just like any other law, so if you are allowed to take a deduction, doesn't it make sense you would take it?

Our very own Supreme Court of the United States once said: "The legal right of a taxpayer to decrease the amount of what otherwise would be his taxes, or altogether avoid them, by means which the law permits, cannot be doubted." (Gregory v. Helvering, 293 U.S. 465).

The law says the Internal Revenue Service must allow you to deduct all "ordinary and necessary" expenses you incur in operating your business. Interestingly enough, the IRS has never actually defined "ordinary" or "necessary." So often only the actual business owner can know if the expense is ordinary and necessary.

Knowing the rules can help you maximize the value of your tax deductions, tax credits, and tax deferral strategies, dramatically increasing the amount of money you get to keep in your own pocket. So let's get started.

BUSINESS STRUCTURES

One of the first areas of concern when thinking about taxes and tax deductions is your business structure. Your choice of a business entity and how you structure the business is one of the most crucial decisions any small business owner should make. Your choice of business entity will have tax implications.

There are advantages and disadvantages to each type so some thought needs to be taken in selecting the right entity that fits your particular situation.

There is no "right" structure. Some structures require more reporting and documentation of decisions than others. Some have more limitations. Some provide more liability protection for the owners. Some structures make more sense in some types of businesses or industries, and do not lend themselves well to others.

Your best course of action is to research the different types and discuss your options with your accountant and a business attorney to make sure you make the right choice for your situation.

The main types of legal structures are:

Sole Proprietor:

Operating as a sole proprietor is the easiest form of business because it is owned and controlled by one person - YOU. There are no official forms to file, no legal requirements to follow, except perhaps for local business licenses, vendor permits, and the like depending on your industry or profession.

You will often be operating under your personal Social Security number unless you hire employees. You are fully responsible for your actions and all actions of employees. If you operate as a sole proprietor, your personal assets are not protected from creditors. If you get in legal or financial trouble with your business or in your personal life, your home, your checking account, and all of your investments are available to creditors.

You cannot deduct any amount you pay on your personal life insurance policy, even if your intention in buying the policy was to allow your family to continue the business in the event of your death. You cannot retain any earnings in a sole proprietorship – every penny you earn is taxable as you earn it.

All income and expenses are reported on Schedule C and incorporated into your individual 1040 tax return. Taxes are paid on the total income of the company, plus any other income sources you may have, not on the business as a separate entity.

You have to pay your own self-employment tax if you earn more than $400 (which you should, or you are really not running a business!). Take it from someone who knows: paying self-employment tax for the first time can be quite an eye-opener.

The amount is roughly equal to twice the amount of Social Security and Medicare tax you would pay as an employee. You know all those deductions that come out of a regular paycheck often labeled FICA? Double that amount and you pay it yourself.

The self-employment tax rate for 2012 is 15.3% (13.3% until February 29, 2012) on the first $110,100 of income and 2.9% on everything above that amount. The first year I paid SE tax, the rate was 25%, so this is an area that has significantly decreased in the past 10 years. Self-employment taxes are reported on Schedule SE and attached to your 1040.

Partnerships:

Two or more individuals or entities can join forces and create a partnership. Partnerships are governed by the laws of each state, so there can be variations between jurisdictions when it comes to establishment, rights, responsibilities, and obligations of partners, and reporting requirements.

But in general, almost every state recognizes two types of partnerships: a General Partnership, where all partners equally share in profits, risks, and responsibilities; or a Limited Partnership, where there are two classes of partners, General Partners and Limited Partners.

General Partners are responsible for their own actions and the actions of employees and actively manage the business. Limited Partners generally do not have an active role in managing the business and have limited responsibilities. Personal assets of General Partners may be open to attachment from creditors, but Limited Partners generally are not.

Partnerships need to establish an Employer Identification Number (EIN) to report their taxes under (see more information below), even if the partners are the only "employees."

Partnerships report their income and all business expense deductions for tax purposes on Form 1065 and each partner receives a K-1, detailing their individual tax liability. Each partner then reports their proportionate share of the partnership's bottom line on his or her individual tax returns.

If a partner has additional business expenses deductions he or she took on an individual basis, they can claim them on an individual Schedule C or on the appropriate line on their individual tax return.

There is another variation of a partnership available in approximately 40 states and several nations around the world called a Limited Liability Partnership (LLP). This entity is often reserved for law firms, accountant practices, architectural firms, medical groups, and other high-risk professions (varies widely by state or country). The main distinction in an LLP is that no individual within the organization can be held responsible for the actions of another individual.

Corporations:

Corporations are the most formally organized business structures and are required to operate under an EIN, not an individual Social Security Number. They are incorporated by one or more individuals who own shares in the organization. Again, state laws govern many aspects of corporations.

Different states and different countries have different rules and regulations. You can choose to incorporate your business in a state other than where you live if you want. Many corporations used to incorporate in Delaware or Nevada because those state laws provided the most benefits and protections for the business owners and limited shareholder rights.

More and more states are moving more toward the Delaware and Nevada models, but it doesn't hurt to check out the differences between states when you are first starting out.

Shares in the corporation may be distributed to and owned by outside interests. Corporations are run by a board of directors and must follow numerous corporate formalities.

If you choose to incorporate, make sure you understand the requirements for documenting decisions, voting rights, and maintaining corporate minute books. Shareholders are not personally responsible for actions of employees and personal assets are widely protected.

Types of Corporations:

Corporations can be C-Corporations (traditional corporation structure) or an S-Corporation, depending on how the organization wishes to be taxed. A C-Corp is taxed on its business earnings and files its own tax return (Form 1120). All deductions are taken at the business level. The corporate tax rate is less than the individual tax rate, so depending on how money from the corporation is dispersed or held for future uses, this type of structure can be appealing in many instances.

Money can be retained at the corporate level, so even though the corporation would have to pay tax on its yearly earnings, the owners can opt to limit or even defer any individual distribution, affecting their individual tax situation.

Each shareholder is then taxed on his or her dividends, or income paid out to them by the company, at their individual tax rate. This is often called double taxation. The owners of the corporation have to pay tax on their company's earnings, and then pay tax again on the earnings that they remove from the company.

Shareholders may not deduct any losses of the corporation on an individual level. Health insurance premiums are deductible to the corporation, as are group life insurance premiums for employee benefits up to $50,000. A C-Corp has no limitation on the number of shareholders.

An S-Corp, on the other hand, does not pay taxes on its earnings. Similar to a partnership, each shareholder will report his or her proportionate share of income, deductions, loss, and credits on his or her individual tax return.

An S-Corp cannot have more than 100 shareholders and no shareholder can be another business entity or foreign. If you plan to be an S-Corp, you must have unanimous consent of all shareholders and you must make the election by filing Form 2553 with the IRS within 75 days of incorporating your business.

If you start out as an S-Corp, you can elect to change to a C-Corp. However, you cannot start out as a C-Corp and then easily change to an S-Corp after the initial 75 days have passed. It can be done, but you'll need a good business law attorney to do it right.

Limited Liability Company:

A Limited Liability Company (LLC) often represents the best of all worlds. They are organized by one or more individuals who are known as members. LLCs have the advantage of protecting personal assets similar to a corporation, but having few formalities to follow.

An LLC can choose how it wants to be taxed. Most choose to be taxed like an S-Corp or Partnership, but some may choose to be taxed like a C-Corp. An LLC must file Form 8832, the Entity Classification Form, and sometimes also a Form 2553 (Election by a Small Business Corporation) and "check the box" to let the IRS know what tax treatment is desired.

If a form is not filed, the IRS will decide for itself how it will consider your tax: If you are a LLC with a sole member, you will be expected to file like a sole proprietor; if you are an LLC with two members, you will be considered a partnership or S-Corp; if you have multiple members, the IRS will consider you a corporation for tax purposes.

An LLC can choose an effective date for tax entity classification. The date can be anywhere between 75 days prior to filing the form with the IRS, up to twelve months after filing for recognition with your state.

LLCs must have an EIN for tax purposes. If the LLC is taxed like a sole proprietorship, all business income and deductions are accounted for on Schedule C of the member's 1040 return. If the LLC wants to be taxed like a partnership, the LLC's income and deductions are reported on a K-1. Taxes are then paid by the individual members on their personal tax returns for their proportionate share of the business income or loss.

Each member must pay his or her own self-employment tax for Social Security and Medicare purposes. If the LLC wants to be taxed like a C-Corp, the LLC will be taxed as a separate entity and the members will only be taxed on their earnings.

Obtaining an EIN

Obtaining an Employer Identification Number is quite easy to do. You can fill out Form SS-4 online at www.irs.gov/businesses/small

and hit submit. You will be issued an EIN immediately upon validation from the IRS. However, a word of caution: the IRS will send a letter in approximately 10 days confirming your number. There have been instances where the online number and the confirming letter contained different numbers.

The confirmation letter is the actual number assigned. If that discrepancy happens to you, make sure you notify every company (usually your bank, accountant, payroll processors) of the change. Otherwise, you will have to clear it up at tax time, which is the worst time to address those types of issues with the IRS.

You can also apply for your EIN via telephone by calling 1-800-829-4933, or simply mailing Form S-44 to the IRS at the address listed on the form.

Establishing the Entity of your Choice

Partnerships, corporations, and limited liability companies are governed by state laws and must be registered with the states in which they do business, have their headquarters, or have a business purpose for registration. In most states, the department that handles those registrations is the Secretary of State, or Department of Commerce.

Most states have their required forms online for you download and complete. Plus, they will give you their filing costs and procedures. You do not need to hire an attorney to file these forms, nor do you need to hire one of those "We Will Incorporate You" firms, unless you want to. The forms and procedures are not difficult to follow, and most states have personnel who are more than happy to answer your questions.

Even though most states do not require it, partnerships should always have a written Partnership Agreement which details who is responsible for what, how disputes (or differences in opinion) will be settled, and what procedures need to be followed when one partner wants out.

Create this document BEFORE there are issues so there are some ground rules for all parties to follow. Once there is an issue between partners, it's way too late to get everyone to sign on the dotted line. You may be best friends when you start the business, but it doesn't mean that you will stay that way forever.

Corporations are required to file a very minimal Articles of Incorporation. To conduct your business properly, you should go the extra step and have Corporate By-Laws drafted. This lays out how the corporation is to be run, how decisions are to be made, what the different categories of shareholders may be and what are their rights.

Again, it's so much easier to have these documents prepared when the company is just beginning instead of waiting until there is a dispute. Plus, there are many documents that are needed on an ongoing basis in a corporation. Never try to run a corporation without a good business attorney being involved.

Limited liability companies, like partnerships, are not required to have any controlling documents except for the registrations with the state, but a good business person will have an Operating Agreement drafted for the LLC, especially if there are two or more members.

RECORDKEEPING BASICS

Once you've established your business entity, now it's time to start to really focus on your documentation and how you are going to keep track of your expenses and deductions.

Getting all of your allowable tax deductions, tax credits, and exemptions all comes down to one thing – documentation. Get in the habit TODAY of detailed, accurate, thorough record-keeping.

You have to find the system that works for you, either recording expenses daily, weekly, or monthly. If you go more than a month without documenting your expenses, you are almost guaranteed to miss out on some deductions. If you spend a dime, write it down. Keep those receipts and make notes on the back of what was purchased.

Make it a habit to look at your receipts before you leave the counter. If the receipt is too vague, ask the clerk for better itemization, especially for any expenses that may have a dual purpose, like a hotel room. If you took your family on your business trip, you will need to show the IRS how much of the hotel bill would have been for just you so you can deduct it.

If you purchase a computer with installed software, you want to know how much of the expense was for the hardware (which has to be depreciated over five years) and how much was for the software (which can be expensed in full the year it is purchased).

All income and expenses records should be kept for a minimum of three years from the date of filing with the IRS. For items that are being depreciated, you need to keep the records quite a bit longer. Some professions (like attorneys and accountants) may have requirements to keep the records longer, too.

If you are depreciating assets, those records should be kept for the lifetime of the asset. You may need that information to determine your basis if you sell or dispose of those assets.

Records on employment taxes paid must be kept for at least four years from the date they were filed with the IRS.

Software

Your choice of a good accounting software program, like QuickBooks or Quicken, can make your life and the life of your bookkeeper and/or accountant so much easier, IF YOU UNDERSTAND HOW THE PROGRAM WORKS. If you don't, trying to use accounting software can be an absolute nightmare.

Remember, the software package is only as good as the data that gets keyed in, so if you are going to be computerized, make sure you keep it updated regularly. Some of the software packages claim to be user-friendly, but most require at least a working knowledge of accounting to fully utilize the features. Most communities have training classes available on different software programs.

If you are unsure what you need and how the software will work for you, take a class, or ask another business owner or your accountant to assist you. Nothing can be more frustrating that having to re-key data or having formulas pop-up and add columns that you didn't want because you don't understand the software. And remember to back-up frequently because losing financial data and then trying to re-create it is a pain. Ask me how I know!

Ledger Books

Many people still choose to keep a handwritten paper trail of their expenses, not just rely on the computer. You can pick up a ledger book at any office supply store. There are several different types, with columns with different types of accounting systems, typically either single-entry or double-entry systems. Pick the one that makes the most sense to you. One good feature of many of the ledger books is that they will have pre-set categories of expenses and often have tax deduction hints and tips that may help you keep on track all year round.

Checkbook Register

Some people choose to keep their checkbook register online. Some banks will even allow you to download your monthly statements directly into QuickBooks or other programs. Whether you keep the register online or a traditional checkbook register, for business purposes, make sure you document what each expense was for. Also, make sure you document where your income is coming from.

Filing Systems

You need to invest in some sort of filing system. It doesn't have to be fancy, just functional. It has to make sense to you and it has to be one that you will use constantly and consistently. An expandable file folder often works well, or you can separate your receipts into different envelopes or different file folders in the drawer.

There are companies out there that will come into your home and set up a filing system for you. Some people like to sort their expenses by month, others prefer receipts sorted by category or classification. Whatever works. And don't be afraid to change your system if what you are doing is confusing or too time-consuming. Keeping good records is the single most important task you can do to save money on your taxes, so treat it like the vital part of your business that it is.

Cash v. Accrual Accounting

There are two basic accounting methods – the cash method or accrual method. The "taxable year" for the cash method is always a calendar year. Corporations using the accrual method can choose to use a fiscal year, which could comprise any twelve month period. Fiscal years can be helpful for businesses that are seasonal in nature, or for a corporation which wants a full year in operation before filing its first tax return. Some accountants will also encourage corporations to select a fiscal year to allow the accountant to work on the company's returns in a less-busy time of the year.

Little known fact: companies which operate on a fiscal year do not have a tax filing deadline of April 15 like individuals. Their tax filing deadline is the 15th day of the fourth month after their fiscal year-end. So if they choose to end their year on June 30, then their tax filing deadline is October 15.

If you are on the cash method, you will deduct expenses in the tax year you pay them and record income when it is received. One drawback to the cash method for service companies is that there are no bad debt losses.

If you perform a service and bill a customer and then never get paid, there is no bad debt to deduct. Under the accrual method, you would have booked the income when you performed the service. Then, when you didn't get paid, you would record it as a loss.

On the accrual method, you deduct expenses when both of the following apply: all events have occurred that fix the fact of liability; and the liability can be determined with reasonable accuracy; and economic performance has occurred.

If your expense is for property or services provided to you, or for your use of property, economic performance occurs as the property or services are provided, or the property is used. If your expense is for property or services you provide to others, economic performance occurs as you provide the property or services.

Generally, under the accrual method, you can deduct an expense as soon as it is incurred or becomes due, whether or not you actually pay the expense at that time (the debt is owed as soon as you receive the bill, not when you send the check). The exception is when the debt is to a person related to you. If that person uses the cash method of accounting, you must actually pay the bill before you can deduct it.

If you are contesting an expense, like a tax dispute, under the cash method, you would take the expense deduction only when you actually pay the disputed amount. Under the accrual method, you can choose to deduct the expense in the year you actually pay the liability or the year that you resolve the contest. More information can be found in IRS Publication 538.

HOME OFFICE DEDUCTION

Eligibility

The general rule is that your personal expenses, including costs of shelter, food, and clothing for yourself is not a tax deduction. But Section 280A of the tax code makes exceptions.

One of the biggest exceptions is that if you work out of your home, apartment or other living quarters, you are eligible for a break on your taxes, so long as you can show that it is your *principal place of business*.

Under IRS rules, your principal place of business is where "you spend the majority of your time and make most of your money." It can also qualify if you use your home for substantial administrative or management activities.

There are two tests that must be met: 1) The business part of your home is used exclusively and regularly for your business or trade; and 2) The business part of your home must be your principal place of business, must be a place where you meet or deal with patients, clients or customers in the normal course of your trade or business, or must be a separate structure (not attached to your home like a garage or studio or greenhouse) used in connection with your trade or business.

You do not have to meet the exclusive use test if the part of your home that you regularly use is for storage of inventory or product samples. There are also special rules for using your home as a daycare facility.

You may also qualify your home as your principal place of business if you use the office exclusively and regularly for administrative or management activities for your trade or business or you have no other fixed location where you conduct substantial administrative or management activities of your trade or business. You can run multiple businesses out of your home office. To claim the Home Office Deduction, you will need to use IRS form 8829 to calculate the amount of the deduction to include on your Schedule C.

If you have more than one business location, determine your principal place of business based on the following factors: relative importance of the activities performed at each location; if the relative importance is not determinative, then consider the amount of time spent at each. Review the IRS regulations in Publication 587.

Room Method vs. Square Footage

There are two IRS-approved methods for determining how much of a deduction you are entitled to take: 1) the Room Method, where you add up the number of rooms in your home and take your home office as a percentage of rooms; or 2) you can use the Square Footage Method, where you add up the square footage of the home and divide by the square footage of the room you are using as the home office.

Since both methods are acceptable to the IRS, you should calculate both and use the one that gives you the biggest deduction. One creative thing to think about – if you are renovating your home room after room, you can move your office into the newly-decorated room and deduct the cost of the paint, flooring, and perhaps other improvements as a business expense. Then next year, move your office into the next room and redecorate. There are no IRS restrictions on how often you change the decor.

Once you've established your eligibility for the Home Office Deduction, you can deduct a percentage of many of your regular household expenses. Many of those are detailed in the Ordinary and Necessary Business Expenses section below.

ORDINARY AND NECESSARY BUSINESS DEDUCTIONS

So, once you have your recordkeeping in place, and you've determined whether or not you can claim a Home Office Deduction, it's time to start collecting your receipts and documenting your expenses.

It is so basic, yet so many small business owners pay taxes needlessly on hundreds, sometimes even thousands, of dollars every year because they fail to keep accurate, thorough records and they fail to recognize a deductible expense. The law says you can deduct **any ordinary and necessary expense that is not extravagant** that you incur in running your business. Your job is to ask yourself before you buy anything: Can this be used to benefit my business? If the answer is yes, then record it. It may be a deduction.

According to the IRS, there are actually over 300 routinely recognized business deduction classifications, yet most business owners claim expenses in fewer than 20 categories. Starting today, make a commitment to yourself to do better than average. Claim every deduction you are entitled to and reap the benefits of more money in your pocket.

Below is a list, certainly not exhaustive, but at least these items should get you thinking along the lines of a true tax-deduction taker:

Rent

If you work out of a leased space, you can deduct your actual rent payments. This includes any CAM (common area maintenance) fees or assessments. If you work out of your home, you can deduct a percentage of your mortgage payment equivalent to the percentage of square footage your home office represents of your home, or by the room method. See the section on the Home Office Deduction for more detailed information.

Telephone Charges

You should have a separate telephone line for your business. That's just good business practice. The IRS will not allow you to deduct the basic telephone charges for your personal home telephone line. However, if you are using your home telephone line, you can still deduct your long distance charges that were incurred for a business purposes (keep good records), or additional charges for voicemail or call forwarding that you incur strictly for your business purposes. Many home-based businesses forget to deduct the monthly charge for voicemail.

Utilities

Typical utility charges include electric, gas, water and sewer fees that are paid above and beyond rent/mortgage. If you are working out of your home, you can deduct these charges at the same percentage as you calculate for your mortgage payments. If you pay for garbage disposal or recycling, don't forget those charges.

Internet Service Fees

If you use the internet for advertising, or research, or have an entirely web-based home business, be sure to deduct these charges. If access to the internet is "necessary" for you to perform your service or provide your product, it's a business expense. However, be careful in today's world of bundled charges.

If you are paying a bundled price for telephone, cable, and high-speed internet, you may not be allowed to deduct the entire amount. However, if you run ads on cable TV, or are running an infomercial, or need to watch a particular program for information vital to your business, you may be able to legitimately deduct your cable bill, and maybe even a portion of that big-screen, high-definition TV (it would have to depreciated as a capital asset, but ...). Again, it would all come down to your record-keeping.

Keep a log that shows when your ad was running, or what programs you watched to keep up on information important to your business. Then log when the television was used for purely personal entertainment. The resulting percentage of those costs can be deducted.

Software Programs

Any upgrades or specialized programs you must purchase, including your accounting software, tax-preparation software, word processor, graphic design package, or whatever you use for your business, can be deducted. If you buy a new computer with installed software, make sure you can identify how much of the purchase price was for the software and how much was for the hardware. The hardware must be depreciated, but the software can be deducted the year it was purchased.

Office Supplies

All office supplies -- paper, pens, staplers, tape, scissors, files, organizers, calendars, waste cans – all of it can be deducted.

Office Decor

The framed artwork, rugs, pamphlet holders, lamps, clocks, anything you purchase to decorate your office can be deducted. If the lamp you purchased for your office gets moved to the guest bedroom when you redecorate, so be it, so long as the original intent was for it to spruce up your office.

Office Furniture

Most of the office furniture you purchase for the business has to be depreciated under the IRS tables (see the section on Depreciation.) However, if you convert items that were for personal use to your business use, you can still deduct them the first year you use them in the business. If you have the original receipts, great, but otherwise, you can estimate the cost (go to a used furniture store, or look in a catalog and take 50% of the retail price) or have an appraisal done. (Note: You can deduct the cost of the appraisal.)

Website Costs

If you paid for a service to design or maintain your website, be sure to deduct those costs. Don't forget your monthly, quarterly or yearly hosting fees, domain name registration and renewal, and any other associated costs.

Advertising/Marketing Efforts

Any efforts expended to promote your business, from the paper to printing, to graphic services can be deducted. If you provide a client with a free sample of your product, it's deductible. If you mail Christmas cards to your clients then the cards, envelopes, and postage is all deductible. And if it so happens that you mail your family and friends your excess inventory because you had to buy the cards in a certain lot size, it doesn't change the deductability. The entire purchase is deductible.

However, if you have custom cards created for specific clients, you can't mail extras of those to your family legitimately. Your costs for stationery and business cards are fully deductible. Costs for running ads is deductible, but so is the mileage you drive to pick-up Chinese food for dinner when you ask the owner to display your flyer on his bulletin board. Even if he says "No" it's deductible. Just be sure to record where you went and who you talked to.

Postage

You can deduct all postage to mail business letters and packages, including delivery and express mail packages. So go ahead and stock up on those Forever stamps for your business.

Credit Card Processing Service Fees

If you accept credit cards, which is an excellent idea for almost any type of business these days, you can fully deduct all of the fees and discounts. And don't forget about PayPal, eBay, Amazon, or Clickbank fees. If anyone else takes a dime of "your"' sale as a processing charge, it's going to be deductible.

Cell phones

Beginning in tax year 2011, as an employer you can provide your employees with a cell phone or reimburse your employees for their use of their personal cell phone for business uses and deduct your costs. This change was made retroactive to 2009, so if you haven't taken a look at your cell phone policy in a few years, now would be a good time. An amended tax return may bring you back some additional money.

As the business owner, you can deduct the entire cost of any cell phone you just strictly for business. If you use one phone for both business and personal needs, then you can only deduct the percentage equal to the business use.

Professional Service Fees

Fees you pay for your bookkeeper, accountant, attorney for legal consultations, financial consultations, any services provided to your business by another professional can be deducted. And that means any other professional. For instance, if you regularly meet with clients at your home and it snows 6 inches overnight, you can hire a snowplow to come and clear your drive and sidewalk as a business expense if you are scheduled to meet with a client that day.

Better yet, hire your 14-year-old daughter – it's still deductible as long as you actually pay her. Or the toilet becomes stopped up and you have to call a plumber during the work day. If your toilet needs to be in working order for your clients, and the rest of your family typically uses the other bathroom, you can deduct your house call. If the toilet is clogged in the main bathroom, then just deduct the same percentage of the fee as your home office deduction.

Copier/Equipment Maintenance Agreement

If you enter into a maintenance agreement for your copier or computer, or even your vacuum cleaner that you use in the business, the costs are deductible.

Banking Fees

All service fees charged by your bank or credit union for your business banking accounts can be deducted, including the monthly service charge, ATM fees for cash withdrawals, even overdraft charges (not that you should have any of those, but still ...).

Cleaning Services

If you hire someone to clean your office on occasion, it's deductible. Even if you are working from home, you can hire a cleaning service. You can then deduct a percentage of your expense – the same percentage as your home office deduction – if they clean your entire home. If they only clean your office area, then it is fully deductible.

Education and Reference Resources (books, newsletters, reference materials)

Trade-related magazines and publications related to your profession or to operating y our business are deductible. For instance, if you paid for this book with the intention of running your business better, then it's a tax deduction. If you regularly run ads, search the newspaper for potential business sources, provide the newspaper to clients as they wait for their appointment with you, or even to scope out competitor's classifieds, your daily newspaper subscription could also be deductible.

Professional Fees / Licenses

If you are a member of a profession, say, an attorney or plumber, you can deduct your costs of maintaining your licensure. However, the costs of obtaining a license for the very first time (i.e. an attorney taking the Bar exam) cannot be deducted.

The rule is that expenses incurred prior to actually being "in business" are preparation costs and are not business expenses. And since an attorney cannot practice law without first passing the state Bar, then those expenses aren't deductible. However, if a practicing attorney takes the Bar exam of a neighboring state, any costs incurred in taking that additional Bar exam would be deductible. Any union dues or trade association dues are fully deductible.

State and Local Taxes

If you are required to pay city, county, or state taxes on your business or business property, these charges are deductible.

Inventory

If you stock and hold products or materials for future sales, you can deduct your expenses to purchase those items and any costs you incur in storing and preserving those items for future sale.

Training Seminars/Online Courses

The cost of education that enhances your knowledge of your business, trade or occupation, or is required by your position, is deductible. You can't deduct education expenses for a career change or to start a new business.

Once the business is started, anything you do to increase your knowledge is deductible. This is a crucial point. START YOUR BUSINESS first, and then you can start deducting.

Child/Dependent Care Expenses

If you pay someone to care for your child under age 13, or a dependent adult so you can work or seek work, you can claim a tax credit for those expenses. The credit is a percentage of your eligible work-related child or dependent care expenses, ranging from 20% to 35%, depending on your adjusted gross income. There is a limit of $3,000 of the expenses paid in a year for one dependent, or $6,000 for two or more.

Bad Debt

If your business loaned money to someone and determined during the tax year that the debtor was going to default and loan is uncollectible, the loss is deductible against business income. For unpaid bills, if you are on the accrual method and you claimed income in one tax year (based on issuing the invoice), that is then determined to be uncollectible in another tax year, you can claim a loss. Cash method businesses cannot claim bad debt losses for unpaid bills.

Interest Paid

Use a credit card exclusively for business, and all interest you paid can be deducted. You can also deduct any annual fees you are required to pay. If you use a credit card for both business and personal expenses, you will have to allocate your interest and annual fees by the dollar amounts charged. If you borrow money for your business, any interest you pay can be deducted.

Depending on your circumstances, you can even loan your business money personally and repay yourself with interest and deduct the interest. You should have an attorney draw up the loan documents to make sure it's done correctly and to preserve the deductibility.

If you take out a loan, perhaps a home equity loan or signature loan, and you use the proceeds for both business and personal reasons, you can deduct the percentage of the interest you paid equal to the percentage of the loan proceeds that were used for the business.

Business Gifts

You can deduct gifts valued up to $25 per person per year, except for gift certificates for food. So if you send Christmas gifs to key clients, or give your staff members items for a special occasion, you can deduct at least a portion of those expenses.

There is no limit on the expense for a gift to another business or corporation so long as the gift is not intended for one specific person. So go ahead and send that basket of goodies to the whole office of your graphic designer (even if it's only her and her husband), and write off the entire expense.

Storage

If you pay a fee to store products or materials, either at a facility or rent a storage unit to sit at your location, those fees are deductible. If you have an empty portion of your basement that you use for storage of materials, you can charge your business a storage fee based on the local market average. Just make sure you document it.

Uniforms

The cost of uniforms or other special work clothes "not suitable for everyday wear" are deductible. Entertainer Liberace once famously deducted his costs for dozens of rhinestone-studded suits – and it was challenged and then allowed by the IRS.

Since many uniforms these days consist of a shirt with a company logo and plain khaki pants, it's more difficult for the IRS to decide what is or is not suitable for everyday wear. It's not a deduction to go crazy on, but hey, a couple golf shirts with your logo tastefully embroidered on the sleeve is also advertising, so you can probably deduct those with no hesitation.

Medical Expenses

You can deduct your out-of-pocket expenses for your medical, dental, and vision care so long as the total exceeds 7.5% of your adjusted gross income. These expenses include your health insurance premiums and all out-of-pocket expenses not covered by insurance. These expenses include prescriptions, over-the-counter remedies, even acupuncture or chiropractic services and the like, so be sure to keep all receipts.

If you get a massage from a licensed massage therapist and the intention is to help you alleviate headaches or release muscle tension, it could be deductible. If you do public speaking as part of your business, have your teeth whitened. It's deductible. The expense has to be for you personally, not your spouse or kids.

If you take every deduction you are entitled to, it's really not that hard to spend at least 7.5% of your Adjusted Gross Income on health-related expenses.

Moving Expenses

If a move is connected with taking a new job that is at least 50 miles further from your old home than your old job was, you can deduct travel and lodging expenses for you and your family and the cost of moving and storing your household goods. If you drive your own car for the move, you can deduct $.235 per mile in 2011. If this is your first job, the 50 mile test applies to the distance between your previous home and your new job.

Professional Associations

You can deduct dues for joining a trade association, your local chamber of commerce, or other professional groups. However, you cannot deduct dues to a social, private, or golf club, unless your business is directly related. So your gym membership probably is not deductible – unless you are a personal trainer and you work with clients at the gym or if you hold client meetings at the gym and you get a discounted rental rate because you are a member. Then you might be able to deduct it. Thinking outside the box is allowed when you are considering taxes.

Charity Donations

You can deduct any cash or noncash contributions your business makes to a qualified nonprofit organization. For instance, you may want to donate one of your products for a charity silent auction. You can deduct the value of that product.

For any cash donation (or gift card), you must have a bank record or written communication from the charity detailing the group's name, the date, and the amount of the donation.

For any noncash contributions over $250 made on one day, you must have a receipt or acknowledgment from the organization. For noncash contributions over $500, you must file Form 8283 with the IRS with your return.

Cost of Goods Sold

If you manufacture goods or purchase them for resale, you generally value inventory at the beginning and end of each tax year to determine your cost of goods sold. Some of your expenses may be included in figuring the cost of goods sold. Cost of goods sold is deducted from your gross receipts to figure your gross profits for the year. If you include an expense in the cost of goods sold category, you cannot deduct it again as a business expense.

The following expenses go into figuring the cost of goods sold: cost of raw materials; freight for delivering raw materials; storage for raw materials; direct labor costs in turning raw materials into final product (including all employee benefit costs); factory or warehouse overhead.

Under uniform capitalization rules, you must capitalize the direct costs and part of the indirect costs for certain production or resale activities. Indirect costs include rent, interest, taxes, storage of final product, purchasing, processing, repackaging, handling, and administrative costs. The rule does not apply to personal property you acquire for resale if your average annual gross receipts for the preceding three (3) years are not more than $10 million.

If you purchased the business, you can look at your predecessor's prior year's gross receipts. For more information, see IRS Publication 334 and Publication 538.

Personal Services to the Business

Many loans require the business owner to personally guarantee the loan or provide the collateral. The business owner (in this case, YOU) can charge the company a fee for this service and the company can deduct the fee as a business deduction. The fee needs to be reasonable and in line with the local market conditions.

Payments-in-Kind

If you provide services to pay for a business expense, the amount you can deduct is limited to your out-of-pocket costs. You cannot deduct the cost of your own labor. Similarly, if you pay a business expense in goods or other property, you can deduct only what the property costs you. If these costs are included in the cost of goods sold, do not deduct them as a business expense.

Casualty Losses

You may deduct losses from storms, floods, fires, or other natural catastrophes to the extent your losses exceed what was covered by insurance plus $100.00, and your losses exceed 10% of your adjusted gross income. If you have not yet collected all of the insurance proceeds, you can estimate your losses. However, you must adjust the amount the following year, either by filing an amended return, or making an adjustment on the next year's taxes, to reflect the actual insurance coverage versus losses amounts. If you have to hire an appraiser to value your losses, you can deduct the fees you paid for the appraisal.

Insurance Deductions

Business and professional liability insurance premiums

Premiums for your business insurance, including property insurance, liability insurance, and equipment coverage are completely deductible. If your profession requires malpractice or other types of specialized insurance, those premiums are deductible.

Disability insurance

If you are self-employed, you should definitely have disability insurance. The premiums are fully deductible, and it's one of the few policies that would pay you back in spades if you needed it.

Automobile Insurance

If your company provides your employees with vehicles for their use for business purposes, or if your automobile is owned through the company, you can deduct the cost of the required insurance. If you choose to take your actual expenses for your vehicle instead of the standard mileage rate, you can deduct a portion of your automobile insurance equal to the amount of time you use the car for business purposes. See the section on Vehicle Expenses for more information.

Health Insurance

Self-employed individuals can deduct up to 100% of the individual health insurance premiums for their own coverage if they are a sole proprietor, in a partnership, or an LLC. If you provide health insurance for your employees, you can fully deduct the costs of all premiums paid.

If you are organized as a corporation, you cannot deduct the health insurance premiums for a policy to cover only yourself.

However, you can get around this by hiring your spouse or kids and providing him or her with a family plan, which happens to cover you, too. Then it's deductible!

Health Savings Accounts

If you have established a high-deductible health insurance plan and are contributing to a Health Savings Account, you can deduct all of your contributions to the account, and it can grow tax-free. Interest earned on a qualified HSA account is not taxed. Funds in an HSA account can be used for any medical, vision, or dental-related expenses.

Beware, though, that using the funds for non-medical reasons can cause a tax liability of 25%. Contributions to an HSA do not reduce your self-employment tax.

MEALS AND ENTERTAINMENT

Deducting Meals

You can deduct 50% of expenses, including taxes and tips, incurred to entertain a client, customer or employees, or anyone from whom you could reasonably expect to be either directly related or associated with your business. You are not required to keep all receipts for expenses under $75, but you should still keep a log of who, where, amount, and when.

You must have a substantive discussion about your business before, during, or after the meal (usually interpreted as being within 24 hours) in order for it to be deductible.

You can deduct the cost of your meal to the extent that it exceeds the amount you would have spent normally. If you routinely go out to lunch and spend $5.00, but when you take a client to lunch, you spend $15.00 on your meal, you can deduct 50% of $10.00, the amount that exceeds your normal expense.

Entertainment Expenses

For entertaining clients at events other than meals, there are some tricky rules. For instance, if you take a client to a hockey game or any other sporting event, your business discussion must take place before or after, but not during, the event.

The IRS says that the business discussion must occur in an atmosphere "conducive" to business. (Caution: the IRS has identified a specific exclusion for membership fees for a golf or athletic club. Your membership fees cannot be deducted as a business expense, even if you conduct a great deal of business on the golf course. But your daily greens fees and cart rental, and the expense of purchasing your clubs, tees, balls, gloves, and shoes, can be business expenses to the extent you use them for business, so be sure to keep records.)

Expenses for an office parties for employees is almost always eligible to be written off completely. Any meals you provide to your employees are deductible, up to the 50% limitation. The exception is for employees who are working overtime. You can provide up to $20 for meals for each day of overtime no more than two times per month.

VEHICLE AND MILEAGE DEDUCTIONS

Record-Keeping Requirement

Almost every business owner knows they should keep careful mileage records if they plan to take a deduction for mileage. The IRS requires your mileage records to be writing. They also expect the entry in your log or journal to be made within seven days of the trip.

Keep a log book in your car and write down the mileage at the beginning of each trip and note the purpose and destination. Another method would be to make sure you write down your mileage in your appointment calendar for every appointment or meeting you attend.

Get into the habit of recording your actual odometer reading on December 31st each year.   Then on December 31st of the next year, you will have a record of exactly how many total miles you have driven.

Deductible vs. Personal Commuting Miles

You will need to allocate your mileage between deductible business miles and non-deductible personal or commuting mileage. Commuting from your home to your principal place of business and back home is non-deductible. You cannot reclassify those miles as business miles, even if you conduct business during your commute (talking on the phone, for instance).   However, once you reach your principal place of business, and then leave to meet with a client, or go to the bank, or take a client to lunch, those miles are business-related and are deductible.

If you are a contractor who goes to a client's place of business to conduct your business activity, and that activity will be completed in less than one year, those can be considered business miles because the client's activity is not your regular place of business.

If you work out of your home, determining what is deductible business miles and what is commuting can be tricky. There have been several Revenue Rulings that have given what seems to be contradictory information.

However, Revenue Ruling 99-7 appears to lay out a good rule of thumb: if you work out of your home and must interrupt your business day for another business activity, it's deductible. If you don't start your business activity until after you've arrived at the other location, it's commuting. For instance, you leave your home to attend a networking event. Is that business or commuting? The rule seems to be that if you simply wake up, eat breakfast and fly out the door to your meeting, then the miles are commuting. However, if you actually conduct some sort of business activity, like checking email or writing a blog post in your home office before you leave, then the mileage is deductible as a business expense.

What if you have a home-based business and a regular 9-to-5 job? Well, it appears that the IRS may allow you to deduct those miles that normally be commuting to your regular job if you conduct your home-based business both before and after work. The key will be your documentation, so keep really good records.

Standard Mileage Deduction Rates

As long as your company is not a C-Corp or S-Corp, you may be eligible to take the standard mileage deduction for any business miles you drive. The standard mileage deduction is calculated by taking the number of business miles driven for the year and multiplying it by the IRS approved standard mileage rate. For 2011 the standard mileage rate was $.555 per mile. Since 2008, the rates have risen twice a year – on January 1 and July 1.

Many business owners only take the standard deduction and don't bother to look any further. For any trips for charitable reasons (donating your time for Habitat for Humanity or serving at a church fund-raiser) you can deduct $.14 per mile for your mileage. This amount has not changed since 2008. For mileage accumulated due to medical reasons (doctor visits, going to the pharmacy to pick up a prescription, etc.), you can deduct $.235 per mile for trips taken in 2011. This rate rose in 2011.

Actual Expense Deduction

You'll want to do a comparison of the standard mileage deduction versus the auto expense deduction to see which way gives you the greatest tax savings. Depending on your vehicle and actual expenses, you may be better off claiming your actual expenses instead of the standard deduction by mileage.

The only way you (or your accountant) will be able to determine which is better is for you to keep your receipts and record ALL of your expenses. The IRS requires you to keep all receipts for expenses more than $75. For expenses less than $75, you need a written record of the expense including where and when it was incurred. All receipts for expenses such as:

- Gasoline
- Oil changes
- Air filters
- Wiper blades
- Radiator flush & fill
- Anti-freeze
- Windshield wiper fluid
- Tire rotation
- Tires
- Car washes
- License plates
- Vehicle registration
- Driver's license renewal
- Automobile insurance premiums
- Car repairs
- Damage to auto not covered by insurance

If your car is used solely for business, then you can also deduct your actual monthly car payments (including your down payment the first year), interest you paid on your car loan, and straight-line depreciation.   If the car is used for both business and personal, then you can deduct the portion of your car payments, interest and depreciation in the same percentage as your business use.

Switching Methods

You should add up all your expenses and compare the sum to the standard deduction. Take the amount that benefits you the most. However, there are limitations to switching from method to method each year, especially if you took the itemized deduction and included any depreciation of the vehicle. You cannot then use the standard mileage deduction method in future years with the same vehicle.

If you started with the standard mileage deduction method, in subsequent years you can switch to the itemized deduction method so long as you only take straight-line depreciation on your vehicle and do not attempt to accelerate the depreciation. Whenever you switch vehicles, you can choose whichever method works best. But make sure you keep good records so if there is ever a question, you or your accountant can be able to explain what went into the calculation each year.

Multiple Cars

And that brings up an interesting scenario – what happens when you use multiple cars in your business?   If it makes sense to itemize your actual expenses for deduction purposes, then in almost all circumstances, if you use multiple cars, you will have a higher deduction.

For instance, instead of simply taking 75% of the expenses for your primary car expenses, by occasionally using your wife's car for your business purposes, you may end up taking 50% of the expenses for your primary car and 30% of the expenses for your wife's car, which in many cases will end up higher. You will need to run the numbers for yourself, but it almost always works out to your advantage.

Parking and Tolls, Public Transportation

No matter which method you use to deduct your mileage, you are always able to claim ordinary and necessary expenses such as parking fees, tolls, car rental, taxis and chauffeurs so make sure you keep your receipts or record these expenses.

Even if you drop a quarter in the meter, you can deduct it – just be sure to document when and where. All garage or parking lot expenses are deductible. However, this does not apply to any parking or speeding tickets – those are NOT deductible under any circumstances. If you have to pay a toll to cross a river or travel a turnpike for work purposes, even if they are for commuting purposes, those costs can be deducted.

Subway, train, taxi, or bus fare used to conduct business is deductible so long as you keep good records. However, you cannot deduct the costs of commuting from your home to your office and back home again using these services.

Owning vs. Leasing

Tax consequences alone should not be the determining factor of what assets to hold in the business, but taxes should be a consideration. When considering whether or not to own or lease a car for your business use, remember that there is a limit on the amount of depreciation you can take under Section 179 if you own the car through the business. Depreciation for the first year is limited to $3,060.00 for 2011. Depreciation on cars often takes 16 years!

But it's different if the car is leased. You can write off the lease expense each year up to the extent you use the car for business. There is no depreciation available. However, you do need to use the car for business for the entire lease. You need to run the numbers both ways to determine what is best for your situation.

There is more information below in the Capitalization and Depreciation section of this book.

Specialty Vehicles

If you purchase a car that runs solely on electric power, you can claim a $4,000 tax credit. If you purchased a sport-utility vehicle or truck to be used in your business with a loaded gross vehicle weight rating of over 6,000 pounds, you can write off all or part of your costs in the first year instead of taking depreciation. For SUVs, the maximum write-off is $25,000. For trucks that have a cargo area of at least six feet in length that is separate from the driver's area, the maximum write-off is $11,260.

Sales Taxes

The IRS has a sales tax table which estimates average sales taxes paid based on region, income, and family size. You are entitled to take the amount estimated by the IRS as a general tax deduction. If you buy or lease a vehicle, you can add any state or local sales tax to the IRS estimate. However, if your state taxes at a rate higher than the IRS estimate, you may not be able to take the entire amount of your additional taxes paid – you may be limited to the IRS estimated percentage.

TRAVEL-RELATED EXPENSES

If you travel for business purposes, both inside and outside the United States, you can often deduct all expenses related to the trip, including transportation, lodging, meals, laundry expenses, cleaning, fax or phone charges.

There are many ways to use this deduction to your advantage. You can combine personal travel so long as the trip is primarily for business (50% or more of your business days are for business purposes). Keep track of your time during normal work days. A work day is considered 4 hours, Monday through Friday, or any day in which you have a business meeting which lasts at least one hour. A travel day is any day in which your travel plus work time equals or exceeds 4 hours. You are not required to take the fastest mode of transportation.

If your business purposes ends on Friday, but your airfare is cheaper if you stay Saturday night, all expenses incurred on Saturday and Sunday morning, even if you are not working, are considered business expenses.

A business trip is defined as traveling away from home overnight on business. That is, you are required to be away from your principal place of business substantially longer than one day's work, and you need to get sleep or rest to meet the demands of your work while away. While on a business trip, you can deduct ALL ordinary and necessary expenses that you incur.

There are two categories of travel expenses – the costs incurred in getting to and from your destination and then the expenses incurred while at your destination.

If traveling within the United States, you can deduct your costs of going to and from your destination will be 100% deductible as long as the trip is primarily for business. That is, your business days out-number the non-business days. However, if the trip is not primarily for business, then none of your costs to and from your destination are deductible. But costs incurred for business purposes at your destination are deductible.

If traveling outside the United States, the rules are slightly different. In order to deduct any portion of foreign travel, the trip must primarily be for business purposes. It will be considered primarily for business if it is either a) 100% for business; b) is less than 8 days, not counting travel days to and from the United States; or c) you spend more than 7 days outside the United States and spend at least 75% of the working hours on business-related activities.

If you meet at least one of these criteria, you can deduct your travel expenses in full. If not, then you need to allocate your travel expenses between your business and personal time.

For expenses incurred at your destination, you can deduct all ordinary and necessary expenses for any business day. However, if the trip is not primarily for business, even your ordinary and necessary expenses are not deductible, except for those directly related to your business.

If you are attending a convention or seminar within the United States, the rules governing business travel in the United States applies. Within North America but outside the United States (a seminar in Cozumel, for instance), if you satisfy the following requirements: show how your business will benefit; there are at least 6 hours of scheduled activities; and you attend at least 4 hours and one minute. The rules for foreign travel apply.

North America includes Canada, Mexico, Puerto Rico, the Virgin Islands, Barbados, Bermuda, Costa Rica, Dominican Republic, Grenada, Guyana, Honduras, Jamaica, Saint Lucia, Trinidad and Tobago.

Outside North America, you can deduct your expenses if you can show that the event is directly related to your business; it was reasonable that it was held outside North America; and it qualifies as a deduction under the foreign travel rules.

The cost of conventions and seminars on cruise ships is deductible, up to $2,000 per year if the events are directly related to your business; the cruise ship is registered in the United States and all ports of call are located in the United States or its territorial possessions; and you attach to your tax return certain documents specified by the IRS (more information can be found in IRS Publication 463).

All receipts for any expense over $75 must be kept. Expenses for less than $75 should be logged in an expense book or otherwise recorded to include purpose for expense, date, and exact amount. If you fail to keep receipts, or it becomes too time-consuming, you can choose to take the standard travel deduction, which can be between $46 and $71 per day, depending on location. You can check the standard amounts that apply by checking the per diem rates at www.gsa.gov.

It is possible to turn your family vacation into a tax deduction with a little planning. While the kids play in the pool, you can check out your competition, learn new business skills, set up referrals, meet with people in the same business to exchange new ideas, attend a seminar, or even try a little job-hunting in the same trade or business.

To make it legitimate, you should do the following: 1) Make contacts, arrangements and have correspondence prior to leaving; 2) Record whom you met, their line of work, what was discussed, how it is expected to benefit your business; 3) Record the nature of your activity; 4) Hand out and collect business cards; 5) Send follow-up letters after you return home; 6) Keep materials from any seminar or convention you attend.

Take Your Spouse and Kids

Your family can travel on business with you. However, their share of expenses, above and beyond what you would have spent if you had traveled alone, cannot be deducted. But if your spouse or kids are employees or their presence is legitimate for the business, their expenses can be deducted, too.

RETIREMENT CONTRIBUTIONS

Contributions to certain qualified retirement accounts, specifically the traditional Individual Retirement Accounts (IRA); Simple Employee Pension Plan (SEP); Savings Incentive Match Plan for Employees (SIMPLE); individual 401-K; Keogh Plans; and other less-common plans specifically created by corporations, can be taken as a deduction on your taxes the year you contribute.

There is also a relatively new product, known as a SUP IRA, specifically designed for self-employed business owners, which can be beneficial to small business owners.

Contrary to the above plans, depending on your circumstances, you may consider contributing to a Roth IRA. Contributions to a Roth are not tax-deductible in the year you contribute, but withdrawals are tax-free.

In very specific circumstances, you may also be eligible for what is called a Self-Directed IRA. This is an investment vehicle that allows you to own investments and assets (like rental properties) within your retirement plan. As the value of the assets grow, so does the value of your retirement plan. Much of that growth is tax free.

You should review your options with a qualified financial planner and your accountant. Your business structure, business income, and number of employees will be important factors in determining what retirement accounts make the most sense for you.

If you are in the 35 percent tax bracket, your taxes would be reduced $350 for every $1,000 you invest in a retirement account. If you can defer your taxes for at least 7 years, you will still be ahead even if you have to withdraw the money early.

Contribution Deductibility Limits

There are, of course, limits on how much you can deduct of your contribute to each type of plan each year. Traditional or Roth IRA, you can contribute up to $5,000 per year if you are under the age of 50, $6,000 if you are older. Contributions to a SEP plan are limited to a maximum of 25 percent of the net income from your business (no minimum).

However, the catch to a SEP is that you have to provide the same plan to all employees if they are over the age of 20 and you have to pay in the same percentage for them as you do for yourself.

SIMPLE Plans can only be set up by companies with fewer than 100 employees. A SIMPLE requires two contributions, one on behalf of the company and one by the employees. Employees can contribute up to $11,500 per year. As the employer, you can choose to either match the employee contribution or contribute a 2 percent of each employee's salary, up to maximum of $4,000. SEP and SIMPLE accounts can be opened or contributed to at any time before you file your tax return (if you have an extension until August 15, you have until August 15 to open or contribute).

Keogh accounts must be opened in the actual year in which the first contribution is claimed, which means that they have to be set up by December 31. Employees must be covered if they work more than 1,000 hours per year and are over the age of twenty-one. You can choose the amount to contribute, up to 13.04 percent of your net business income, or a maximum of $22,500.

There are two types of Keogh accounts – profit-sharing and money purchase. Contributions to a money purchase account may be up to 20% of the company's net income, or 25% of your net minus one-half of your self-employment tax, up to a maximum of $30,000. You have to choose the amount to contribute to the profit-sharing Keogh. You can pair Keoghs, own both a money purchase and a profit-sharing, so you can maximize your contributions.

The rules for a Self-Directed IRA are very complex and specific. Research these thoroughly before investing.

In most retirement account instances, the taxes are deferred until you withdraw the funds. Beware: some early withdrawals will be taxable at your then-current rate and you will incur a 10% penalty. An early withdrawal is considered any withdrawal before you are the age 59 ½, with some exceptions.

You can often withdraw money from retirement accounts before age 59 ½ if you are disabled or if you have medical expenses which exceed 7.5 percent of your adjusted gross income. There are also certain circumstances when you can withdraw money to purchase a first home, or for higher education for you or your family members.

Pension/Retirement Plan Start-Up Costs

Small companies, with fewer than 100 employees, are allowed a tax credit for up to 50% of the cost of establishing a new retirement plan. The maximum credit per year is $500.00.

CAPITALIZATION AND DEPRECIATION

Some purchases cannot be deducted as a business expense because they are considered to be Capital Assets of the business. These are items that the IRS has determined have a useful life of more than one year. Capitalized assets are accounted for differently than other assets in terms of where and how they are reflected on your income/balance sheets.

Start-Up Costs

During your first year of operation, you can deduct $5,000 of the costs you incur to get started. These expenses include fees for business set-up, legal consultations, office furniture, etc. Or you can choose to amortize these costs equally over 5 years. The choice is yours. If you need maximum deductions in year one, take it all. Otherwise, spread it out so that you will have at least 20% worth of deductions in each of the next 4 years.

Additionally, you can deduct up to $25,000 worth of business equipment that would be considered fixed assets (computers, printers, machinery, tools of the trade, etc.) during your first year of business instead of depreciating the assets according to the IRS schedules (more on depreciation tables later).

Depreciation

The concept of depreciation is pretty simple. Almost every asset decreases in value over the time. The exceptions include land, some diamonds and gemstones, precious metals, and other collectibles. Almost everything else can be counted on to lose value over time.

To make things consistent for everyone, the IRS has pre-determined a useful life for many several categories of products. All assets must be depreciated according to its class. There are 6 basic schedules: 3-year property; 5-year property, 7-year property; 10-year property; 15-year property; and 20-year property. For instance, computers are considered to be 5-year property, so the cost of the hardware must be taken over a 5-year period. IRS Publication 534 gives much more detailed information on the categories and tables.

First Year Conventions

In the first year that you purchase an item, if it is not deducted as a Start-up cost, you will need to know when in the year it was first used in the business. There are three accounting "conventions" that are commonly used – you should pick the one that gives you the biggest benefit.

The half-year convention says that all assets purchased in year one were in service by the middle of the first year. Under that assumption, you would only take one-half of the first year depreciation for each item, which would then allow larger depreciation values in later years.

The mid-quarter convention should be used if the majority of the purchases are made during the last three months of the year. Under this rule, each item purchased before April 1 would be depreciated at 87.5% of its value; items purchased in April through July 1 would be depreciated by 62.5%; items purchased between July and September would be depreciated at 37.5%; and the remaining items depreciated at 12.5%.

The final rule would be the mid-month convention, which would take every item purchased and figure the depreciation value for each item. The assumption is always that the item was put in service on the 15th of the month it was purchased. This is the most accurate, but also the most complicated convention. Good record-keeping is vital for these calculations.

Calculating Depreciation

Once you have identified the items that need to be depreciated, you need to determine what property class it falls under for IRS purposes. You then decide what convention to use. In most instances, you will use what is called Straight Line depreciation, where you take the cost of the item, find the MACRS (Modified Accelerated Cost Recovery System) classification table that applies to your property class, and multiply by the percentages provided by the IRS.

However, in some instances, your accountant may recommend that you use the Double Declining Method (sometimes called the 150% Method) to depreciate items faster. You can use either method so long as you are consistent.

Section 280F Depreciation Limits

Section 280F limits the amount of depreciation you can take for vehicles, especially passenger cars, used in your business. There are so many variables you really should go over your situation with a tax professional in order to determine how much depreciation you can take for vehicles you use in your business. Many specialty vehicles, like delivery trucks, tractors, qualified moving vans, taxis, school buses, and ambulances, have no limit on depreciation limits under Section 280F.

Section 179 Deductions

Wait! There's more. If you purchase equipment, including office furniture, copiers, computers, printers, or whatever and can't take all of your first year purchases as Start-Up costs, do you have to depreciate it? Not if it can qualify as a Section 179 deduction.

To qualify as a Section 179 deduction, your purchase must meet four criteria: 1) The asset must be tangible and not real property or an improvement to real property; 2) The asset must be used in the business the year it is purchased. Therefore, you generally cannot deduct items that you have converted from personal use to business use. These items must be depreciated; 3) You must take the Section 179 deduction in the first year the asset is used; and 4) The asset is used at least 50% of the time to benefit the business and not for personal uses.

If the asset is used for personal uses, you can only deduct the percentage of the cost equal to the percentage of its use for business.

Section 179 deductions are limited to $350,000 worth of assets for tax year 2011. If you have more costs than the maximum, you can deduct the maximum, and then depreciate the rest according to the IRS tables.

CAUTION: Many states have established their own rules regarding what can deducted under Section 179. Make sure you check your state laws because their depreciation tables and maximum amount may differ.

Cost Segregation

Cost Segregation is a strategic tax tool that allows companies which have constructed, expanded, or remodeled real estate to accelerate their depreciation deductions. The process involves commissioning an engineering report that meets IRS standards. Only a professional company who understands the IRS requirements should be hired. Make sure your CPA understands the process, too.

The engineer must classify all components of the construction into four categories: personal property, land improvements, building components, and the land. The standard depreciation timeframe for real estate purchased for business purposes is a straight-line depreciation schedule over 39 years.

By segregating the construction project into categories, many areas may be depreciated over as few as five years, greatly accelerating the depreciation. Items categorized as personal property include things like furniture, carpeting, window treatments, etc. These items have a much shorter useful life than 39 years, and can be depreciated at either a 5-year or 7-year rate.

You can also use the double-declining method, shortening the depreciation period even more. Land improvements include items like landscaping, sidewalks, fences, etc. These can be depreciated over a 15-year period and can be depreciated at a 150% declining method.

Buildings often can be broken into different components so that, if one part, say, a roof, becomes obsolete prior to the end of the 39-year depreciation schedule, the remaining value in that individual component can be written off immediately. Whatever value is left over that is not accounted for in the first three categories is attributed to the land. Land itself is not depreciable.

Even previously-acquired property can be cost segregated with the required engineering reports. The IRS will allow you to look back up to 10 years. You must file IRS form 3115 in order to apply the accelerated depreciation to previous returns. The drawback to cost segregation is the cost of the engineering study, often $15,000 or more. But the tax benefits of the study are almost always worth it. And the study itself is an allowable business deduction. Most studies can be completed in four to six weeks.

Another potential disadvantage to be aware of is if the real estate is only going to be held a short time. There may be some tax recapture provisions to be considered. But if you own real estate in your business, cost segregation should be looked at for some additional tax savings over straight depreciation.

Energy-Efficiency Improvements

An exception to the rule that improvements to property have to be depreciated exists for improvements which decrease a commercial building's energy usage by 50% or more, including insulation, energy-efficient windows and doors, etc. These expenses can be deducted immediately rather than depreciated.

The deductible amount cannot exceed $1.80 per square foot of floor space. If the savings is between 16.67% and 50%, the maximum write-off is $.60 per square foot. This deduction was scheduled to be eliminated in 2008, but has now been extended through tax year 2009.

EMPLOYEES

In every small business owner's life, there comes a time when hiring help is considered. Whether your decision is to hire an employee or contract with an independent contractor to assist you, it's a big step – and not one that should be taken lightly.

Managing payroll and correctly remitting payroll taxes should be left to professionals, or expect to spend a lot of your available time in making sure it's right. It is easy to make mistakes if you don't understand the processes and timeframes.

Required Forms

If you are going to have employees, you will to make sure an Employee Eligibility Verification form (Form I-9) from the United States Immigration and Naturalization Service for each employee hired. A new form was issued in January, 2008, so all hires after that date should use the new form. These forms need to be retained by the employer for three years after hire, or at least one year beyond termination.

Almost every state also requires that you report all new hires in the state, usually within 14 to 30 days of hire. These forms typically report an employee's name, address, Social Security number, date of birth, date of hire, and place of employment. This information assists the state in collecting outstanding child support, reduces fraudulent worker's compensation and unemployment claims. In addition, every employee must complete a federal W-4 form.

Expenses your business incurs by having employees are fully deductible, including their salaries /commissions, the Social Security taxes you pay on their behalf, payroll taxes and fees, workers compensation fees, unemployment insurance fees, and more.

Businesses can deduct the cost of fringe benefits provided to employees, such as health insurance, retirement accounts, or company cars. Also, any prizes or awards given to employees can be deducted. Providing employees with company-paid financial advice is a good tax deduction as well as a valuable fringe benefit.

Independent contractors

If you pay any individual or company more than $600 per year, you must issue a 1099 and report the payments to the IRS. You can then deduct those payments as an expense and the IRS will look for that money on the individual's tax return.

Sometimes, you want help with your business, but don't want employees. Consider independent contractors. The advantages of using Independent Contractors include no payroll taxes, including Social Security, Medicare, unemployment insurance, or workers compensation costs. There is also a lot less paperwork.

Because employers do not pay Social Security and Medicare taxes, or contribute to the unemployment coffers or pay into workers compensation funds for independent contractors, the IRS would like to classify all workers as employees and are skeptical of companies who conduct the majority of their business using independent contractors.

The IRS has developed twenty factors which small business owners must take into consideration in determining whether or not your hired help is indeed independent or if they are actually an employee.

The twenty factors are:

1) Must the worker comply with the employer's instructions about when, where, or how to work?

2) Does the worker receive employer-supplied training?

3) Does the worker provide services that are an integral part of the business?

4) Must the worker render services personally?

5) Does the worker hire, supervise, and pay assistants for the employer?

6) Must the worker follow set hours of work?

7) Does the worker work full time for the employer?

8) Does the worker work on the employer's premises?

9) Does the worker perform tasks in an order of sequence set by the employer?

10) Must the worker submit oral or written reports?

11) Is the worker paid by the hour, week, or month?

12) Is the worker furnished with tools and materials?

13) Does the worker work for only one employer at a time?

14) Can the worker be fired, other than for breach of contract?

15) May the worker quit without incurring liability to the employer?

16) Does the worker have a significant investment in the service-provided facilities?

17) Can the worker realize a profit or loss?

18) Does the worker make services available to the general public?

19) You should have a written contract with an independent contractor, which specifies their job responsibilities and terms of your engagement.

20) Does the contractor runs his business like a business, with proper licenses and insurance. Insist that your contractor provide you with invoices, and make sure your payments to the contractor are made payable to the contractor's business, not to them personally.

Hiring Family Members

Hiring your family members may be a consideration, especially your teenagers because they have a lower tax bracket. Just make sure they perform bona fide services. Depending on the amount of wages, your child may pay no taxes at all. For children under age 18, there are no FICA payments.

If your spouse regularly helps you stuff envelopes, or does your filing, or even proof-reads your correspondence, pay them for it. Put them on payroll. You can then deduct their salary, including any benefits and taxes you pay for them, as a business expense. HINT: Pay them monthly. Less paperwork, less tax, more time to gather money.

If you provide a family health insurance plan, you can deduct the expense. The business can provide up to $50,000 in life insurance coverage, with the premiums fully deductible.

TAX CREDITS

As opposed to a deduction, which is used to reduce your income upon which tax is calculated, a tax credit reduces your tax liability directly. Don't forget to consider the possibility of a tax credit when making business decisions.

Employment Credits

One way a small business owner can gain a tax credit is to hire disabled or minority employees (work opportunity credit, empowerment zone credit, etc.) Check with your state employment agency on whether it can assist you. If your business is near an Indian reservation, you can get a tax credit for any wages you pay to members of a tribe.

Childcare Facilities

If you build a day care facility to care for the children of your employees, you can claim a tax credit for up to $150,000 per year for the costs of the building and operating the facility.

Community Development Corporations

If you invest in a CDC selected by the federal government, you can get a tax credit for 5% of your investment for the first ten years of your investment.

Disabled Access Credit

For companies with gross incomes of less than $1 million or employed fewer than 30 workers, you can claim a credit, up to $5,000, for improvements you made to your facility to make it handicapped accessible, including adding ramps, enlarging doorways, remodeling bathrooms.

Low-Income Housing Credit

If you are a real estate investor financing projects primarily for low-income housing needs, you can claim a tax credit.

New Markets Tax Credit

Local and state governments often have incentives for investments in companies which will lend money to firms in poor areas. Investors get a 5% credit in the first three years on the money they put up and a 6% credit for the next four years.

Passive Activity Credit

Credits from investments in activities you don't materially participate can only be used to offset any tax due on passive income. Excess credits earned in the first year can be carried over to the second year.

Rehabilitation Credit

If you purchase an historic building, you can get a tax credit for up to 20% of the cost of renovating it. The renovations must be completed within 24 months, and must meet all governmental standards.

Energy-Efficient Renovations

There is a whole slew of credits available to businesses which renovate buildings using energy-efficient materials, including windows and doors, insulation, air conditioning units, furnaces, roofs, heat pumps, geo-thermal appliances, water heaters, fuel cells, and solar energy or wind-powered systems.

STRATEGIES TO MANAGE YOUR TAXES

Review Your Tax Return Before Filing

It seems like common sense, but do not hit "submit" or let your accountant or tax preparer submit your returns before you have had a chance to thoroughly review the completed return.

Here are some common mistakes that you should be sure to avoid: 1) Failure to sign the return. Make sure you follow the procedures for attaching your electronic signature if submitting online; 2) Mathematical mistakes; 3) Incorrect social security number; 4) Mistake in routing or account number for direct deposit; 5) Failure to include payment for taxes when required; and finally, 6) Missing the filing deadline.

Pay Your Estimated Taxes

One of the responsibilities of the self-employed is to pay your estimated taxes on a quarterly basis (April, June, September, and January). You are required to pay an estimated tax if you expect to owe most than $1,000 to the IRS in a given tax year.

There are two methods of determining how to pay your estimated taxes: if you expect to earn approximately the same amount as last year, you should pay the amount that was owed last year. If you did not make a profit last year and didn't pay any tax, you will not be required to pay any estimated taxes this current year. You must pay 90% of your taxes due for the current year, or 100% of the previous year's taxes.

If you don't make any money during the first quarter of the year (January through March), then you do not have to make an estimated payment on April 15. If you don't make any money prior to June, you do not have to pay on June 15, as so on.

If you filed a 1040 last year, you should have received 1040-ES estimated tax payment vouchers.

File for an Extension if You Need It

Formally request an extension if you need it to avoid late filing penalties. You can get up to six more months (until October 15) by filing Form 4868. Penalties can be substantial, ranging from 6% to 8% annually. The penalties begin to accrue on the date your estimated taxes become unpaid.

Review Previous Returns and Amend as Necessary

A lot of people believe that once a tax return is filed, your missed deductions are lost. NOT TRUE! You can amend your tax returns for three years after the filing date. So pull out those old tax returns and review. If you find new deductions, go ahead and file an amended return.

Manage Timing of Purchases and Income

The timing of your purchases and the collection of income can affect your taxes. You can work with your vendors to pay them in advance for work expected to be completed during the next year, or delay sending out bills at the end of the year so the income is not recordable in this year. But beware: you generally cannot deduct fixed or regularly-occurring expenses in advance, even if you pay them in advance.

This rule applies to both the cash and accrual methods. It applies to prepaid interest, prepaid insurance premiums, and any other expense paid far enough in advance to, in effect, create an asset with a useful life extending substantially beyond the end of the current tax year.

If you claimed an expense in one tax year, and then recovered that same expense in the next year, it needs to be deducted from the next year's expenses. If you had an expense and recovery in the same year, the recovery needs to be offset against the expense prior to calculating your deduction for the year.

LIMITS ON LOSSES

If your deductions for an investment or business activity are more than the income it brings in, you have a loss. There may be limits on how much of the loss you can deduct.

Not-for-Profit Limits

If you carry on your business activity without the intention of making a profit, you cannot use a loss from your non-profit to offset other income.

At-Risk Limits

A deductible loss from a trade or business or other income-producing activity is limited to the investment you have "at risk" in the activity. You are at risk in any activity for the following: money and adjusted basis of property you contribute to the activity; amounts you borrow for the use in an activity if you are personally liable for repayment; or you pledge property (other than property used in the activity) as security for the loan.

Passive Activities

Generally you are in a passive activity if you have a trade or business activity in which you do not materially participate, for example, you own an apartment building but use a management company. In general, deductions for losses from passive activities only offset income from passive activities. You cannot use any excess deductions to offset any other income.

In addition, passive activity credits can only offset the tax on passive income. Any excess loss or credits are carried over in later years. Suspended passive losses are fully deductible in the year you completely dispose of the activity.

Net Operating Losses

Carry back the loss to generate an immediate tax refund. Or, if you anticipate greater profits in the future that will put you into a higher tax bracket, consider waiving the net operating loss carryback and carrying your loss forward to the next tax year. Net Operating Losses can be carried back for two years unless you specifically elect to carry them forward. Be sure to keep track of NOLs from year to year.

SPECIAL TAXES

Self-Employment Tax

The Self-Employment Tax (SEA) is a creature all its own. It is not an income tax per se – you can owe no taxes, or even be entitled to a refund, and still have to pay your self-employment tax. The SEA is how self-employed individuals pay into the Social Security and Medicare funds. Unfortunately, the rate that self-employed taxpayers pay is the highest the IRS allows.

You are responsible for paying SEA if you earn at least $401 from your business, whether you work fulltime or part-time. There are also special rules for income from non-profits, so make sure you check if that is your situation.

One-half of your self-employment tax is taken on the front of your 1040 as an adjustment to income, which reduces your adjusted gross income.

Special note on adjustments made to self-employment taxes: If you must amend your tax returns and the new returns increase the amount of tax you paid (which in turn, increases the amount you pay into the Social Security trust fund for yourself), you must amend your return within 3 years, 3 months, and 15 days after the tax year you are amending ended (December 31). After that time, you still have to pay the correct amount of tax, but the SSA will not credit your account. But they will deduct from your account with no time limit at all. Nice to know, isn't it?

Alternative Minimum Tax

The alternative minimum tax (AMT) is a highly controversial additional tax that was originally intended in the 1970s to prevent the ultra-wealthy from using special tax shelters and tax strategies to pay little or not tax. The tax law has not kept up with reality, so what started out as a tax on fewer than 20,000 people in its first year of enactment now affects millions of regular taxpayers.

The AMT is actually a separate tax system that is in addition to your regular business or individual income tax. If you or your business has a gross income of higher than $75,000, you may very well be caught in the AMT trap. Basically, to figure your potential AMT liability, you must complete Form 6251.

Some software programs can do this for you, but if you are doing your return by hand, it would be best to have a professional tax preparer complete this form for you. Many of the deductions you are allowed for regular income tax purposes are added back in, expenses such as employee expenses deducted from your business income, and medical and dental deductions.

The AMT exemptions in 2006 were $62,550 for joint filers and $31,275 for single taxpayers. However, these exemptions are reduced by 25% of each dollar over taxable income over $150,000 for couples, or $112,500 for singles. The AMT tax rate is 26% on the first $175,000 of income and 28% on any excess. If the AMT calculation results in a higher tax than your normal income tax, you are required to pay the higher amount.

However, there could be one silver lining – if you are forced to pay the AMT in one year, you may be eligible for a tax credit in future years up to the amount you paid AMT over your regular income tax. You will need to complete Form 8801 to see if you meet the criteria.

For more information on the AMT rules, you can read IRS Publication 909.

DO-IT-YOURSELF vs. HIRING EXPERTS

Tax Preparation Software

Tax preparation software makes it much, much easier for the small business owner to do his or her own taxes. There are dozens of choices, with new packages being made available every year. But beware, not all tax-preparation software packages are alike.

Your first step should be to evaluate your personal situation. Make sure the package you select can handle the variations you need for your business. Feel free to comparison shop online and at your local office supply or media supply store. Some packages include state forms, some do not. Some are very hands-on, tutorial-based programs, while others assume a strong basic knowledge of tax filings with bare-bones instructions.

Most software programs provide support through an 800# and online help. Some will even provide you with assistance in an audit situation. Some include online filing with the base cost, some charge extra. Price should be only one of your considerations ... considering the ease of use and appropriateness for your situation are just as important.

No matter what package you use, make sure you print out a copy of the return and review it carefully before submitting to the IRS. Some packages have an "error check" or "audit flag" feature. Make sure you run it. Just because a flag is raised, it doesn't necessarily mean your deduction or entry is wrong, but make sure you are comfortable with your reasoning as to why you feel you can claim it.

If your deductions are ever challenged by the IRS and you did your return yourself, you need to be confident that you have the appropriate documentation and logical support for any questionable deduction you may take.

If you have complications in your taxes you are unsure about, you may want to have your do-it-yourself returns reviewed by a tax professional before you submit it. The cost may be well worth it, and it's a tax deduction, so make sure you claim it.

As a small business owner, your time and personal resources can often be more effectively used to *make* money and work on your business than to spend hours completing tax returns. Finding a competent, reliable tax professional, or even a good bookkeeper, can free you from the burden of staying absolutely on top of all changes in the tax code, and will free you from the drudgery of completing your own returns.

The IRS says it takes the average individual 13 hours to complete a personal tax return. It can be twice as long for the typical business owner. Looking for a tax professional is a lot like looking for a dentist, a family doctor, or an attorney. The best place to start is to ask your friends, neighbors, or business colleagues for recommendations.

Especially talk to accountants who are working with businesses similar to yours. You should try to get a list of three or four possibilities, and then set up interviews with each. Be sure to tell them that you are searching for a professional and just want to meet with them and ask some questions before committing. Be sure to ask about their consultation fees. Some will offer free consultations, other will not.

There are typically five categories of tax professionals to consider: storefront tax preparations shops; independent tax preparers/bookkeepers; enrolled agents; certified public accountants; and tax attorneys.

Storefront Tax Preparers

Let's first look at storefront tax preparation shops. Their workers are usually seasonal employees and, though they have been through more training on taxes than you may have personally, they don't know your business and you can rarely develop a long-term, trust-based relationship. They can be very efficient at straightforward, relatively simple returns.

These employees often cannot represent you before the IRS or in tax court, but they can accompany you to an audit if needed to answer questions on the return they completed. Many of the services also provide a guarantee or you can buy a "peace of mind" promise for an additional fee. It's usually worth the price.

The IRS is instituting a Registered Tax Preparer test, which all storefront or independent tax preparers will need to pass by December, 2013. After that time, make sure you verify that they are registered with the IRS before trusting them with your taxes.

One service that several of the storefront tax preparers offer is that they will review your previous year's returns and look for errors, often for free or for a minimal charge. Take advantage of that offer when you see it. Another set of eyes is never a bad idea. If they find a mistake, they will charge you a fee to file the amendment. If the revised refund is more than the fee, then it's probably worth it.

One note: If you use a storefront tax preparation service, make sure you insist that they provide you with your original documents and a complete copy of your filed return. Many of them will offer to keep your documents as a "service." Don't fall for it – they just want you to return so they are there to offer their services when a tax question or issue arises.

Independent Bookkeepers as Tax Preparers

Many bookkeepers are willing, and perfectly capable, of preparing taxes for their clients. But some are not trained in taxes and only have a cursory understanding of the tax law. Once the IRS Registered Tax Preparer test is instituted, we may see many of the smaller, less qualified shops go out of the tax preparation business.

Enrolled Agents

An enrolled agent is licensed by the federal government and is often a former IRS employee. Many storefront tax preparers employ Enrolled Agents to handle more complex returns. At the very least, an enrolled agent has passed a comprehensive IRS exam. Enrolled agents, however, often specialize in certain types of businesses, so be sure to ask about their experience. Enrolled agents can represent you before the IRS and during an audit, but generally not in tax court, unless they are also an attorney.

Certified Public Accountants

A Certified Public Accountant (CPA) is licensed by the State and has been tested on various areas of accounting procedures, though not all are tax specialists. They are required to take regular continuing education courses to stay current on accounting procedures and tax law. The strength of a CPA is his or her ability and training to look at the bigger picture and assist in unraveling complex financial issues.

CPAs can represent you before the IRS and in audits. Just a note: don't completely ignore those recent accounting graduates who haven't yet passed their exam. They may be able to assist you at the beginning of their career, and at a significant discount.

Tax Attorneys

Tax attorneys are generally knowledgeable about complex, corporate issues. They will often know the latest laws and issues in tax disputes, but may not be as conversant on the actual completion of the actual tax return. They can represent you before the IRS, during an audit, and appear before the tax court if the dispute goes beyond the IRS auditor or field office.

Characteristics to Look For

The characteristics for the right tax professional for you is one who a) understands your business; b) understands your income and expenses; c) is neither overly aggressive nor unreasonably conservative; d) is competitively priced; e) is not too busy to take on a new client; f) can be reasonably available to spend some time with you and answer your questions and provide you with advice; and most importantly, g) is someone you are comfortable with, someone you can talk to, someone you can trust.

Be aware that some tax professionals and CPAs are only in business for part of the year. You really should look for a full-time professional, not someone who only does taxes during tax season.

Make sure you inquire as to what services your chosen professional provides. Some CPAs will set up accounting software for you, or will reconcile your monthly bank statements, or will even provide basic bookkeeping services such as writing checks to your vendors. Be sure to ask. They will often have contacts with payroll services, check-printers, and bankers, so they are often good resources for other business needs.

PREPARE FOR AN AUDIT

It happens to thousands of Americans every year – a notice from the IRS that their tax returns are being audited. But rest assured, only about 2% of small businesses are audited in any given year. If it happens to you, here are some tips on how to handle it with minimal anxiety. There are three types of audits: the correspondence audit, the audit at a local IRS agent, or a field audit.

Correspondence Audit

The correspondence audit is the easiest. It is typically just a letter from the IRS seeking clarification of a certain entry. A straightforward reply will typically answer their question and it will be over. Your return is not under strict scrutiny, there is just a question.

In-Office Audit

When you receive a request to appear at an IRS office, your return is being reviewed more thoroughly. Typically, when you show up at the interview, the IRS agent shows up with a pretty thin file. They'll have a copy of the tax return to be audited, your tax-filing history for the past six years – and a list of all third-party payments made to you or reported on W-2s and 1099 forms. That's all. Everything else they want to learn from you. Your notice should include a list of items that the auditor wishes to review.

First rule of thumb when dealing with an IRS auditor – don't volunteer information. They will ask for many things they are not legally entitled to, for instance, copies of bank statements for personal accounts, property deeds, or police reports. You are only obligated to provide records that deal specifically with an item or items on the tax return being audited.

Anything accounted for on a previous year's return, or non-taxable items, are not required to be revealed. Don't feel pressured. It's okay to say "No" to an IRS auditor. If the auditor really thinks there is a problem with another year's tax return, he can request it from the IRS records. If he hasn't, then the auditor is just fishing for information.

You do not need to provide anything extra. If the audit notice states that the auditor is questioning certain deductions, be prepared with documents relating to those specific deductions, no more.

Field Audit

Finally, there is the field audit. This will be conducted at your principal place of business or home and everything can be fair game. Many people consider this to be as much a "lifestyle" audit as a review of your taxes. The IRS agent will be attempting to ascertain if your lifestyle matches your tax returns.

If you are summoned for an audit, you may consider hiring a professional representative, either your tax preparer or an attorney, to meet with the auditor on your behalf.

You can complete the IRS power of attorney, form 2848, so that your representative will get all of the notices and can communicate with the agency on your behalf. Your representative should have only the bare facts, and cannot reveal personal information. They are not emotionally involved and can negotiate and respond professionally.

For items that need more clarification, the representative will ask the auditor to put them in writing. Then, you and your representative can answer those concerns as narrowly as possible.

If you are confident in your ability to face the IRS yourself, you certainly have that right. You should thoroughly review all of your returns, schedules, and organize your receipts. You have the right to request a delay if you need more time to prepare. Don't feel unduly pressured. If you appear organized at the audit interview, the auditor will be more likely to believe that you were organized when you completed your taxes. It would be wise if you at least ask a tax preparer or attorney to review your documents and prepare you for the audit interview.

Also, the IRS provides their agents with audit guides, which are available for review online, so it may be wise to pull up the guides so you know what the agents have been instructed to ask. Oh, and by the way, fees paid to your tax preparer or attorney for preparing you or defending you at an audit are tax deductible.

HOBBY/NOT-FOR-PROFIT ACTIVITIES

Treat your hobby as a business and if you lose money, you can deduct it. However, if you make money, you have to treat it as income.

If you do not conduct your business in a business-like manner, you run the risk of having the IRS determine that you are actually participating in a hobby and not a business. If that happens, you cannot deduct any losses.

To determine whether or not you are participating in a hobby or are running a business, the IRS looks at several factors, no one of which is determinative, but are looked at overall.

These factors include: 1) You carry on the activity in a business-like manner; 2) The time and effort you expend indicates that you intend to make it profitable; 3) You use the income derived from the activity to support yourself or your family; 4) Your losses are due to circumstances beyond your control; 5) You make changes to your business in order to improve profitability; 6) You have the knowledge necessary to make a profit in this area of endeavor; 7) You have made a profit in similar activities in the past; 8) You have made a profit in some years with this activity; 9) You can expect to make a profit beyond just the appreciation of assets involved in the activity.

If an activity has made a profit in at least 3 of the last 5 years, it is considered an activity for profit. There's an exception for businesses consisting of breeding, training, showing, or racing horses: those activities are presumed to be profitable if the business has made a profit in 2 of the past 7 years. The activity needs to be substantially the same during those 5 (or 7) years.

If the taxpayer dies before the end of the 5-year (or 7-year) period, the test period ends on the date of the taxpayer's death. If the business passes the profitability test, there are no limitations on the business expenses or losses you can deduct from your taxes.

What happens when you haven't been in business long enough to pass the IRS test? You can file Form 5213, which will postpone any determination that your business is intended to make a profit until 5 years (or 7 years) have passed after you began your business. The benefit of filing this form is that the IRS will not question your business losses or restrict your deductions until after you have completed your fifth (or seventh) year.

However, if you do not make a profit in 3 of those 5 years, the IRS can retroactively limit your losses and deductions. Form 5213 must be filed within 3 years of the due date (April 15th) of your tax return for your first year in business.

If you file your tax return and receive a notice from the IRS that they are disallowing deductions for your business, you have 60 days to file Form 5213. Filing Form 5213 automatically extends the period of limitations on any years in the 5-year (or 7-year) period to 2 years after the due date of the last return.

If your business is deemed to be a not-for-profit endeavor, you can only deduct expenses in the following categories up to the extent allowed:

Category 1: Standard deductions on your Schedule A attached to your individual 1040 tax return. You can only deduct a casualty loss on your personal property only if the loss is more than $100 and exceeds 10% of your adjusted gross income.

Category 2: Any deductions that do not result in a basis of property, only to the extent of your gross income from that activity that is in excess of the deductions in Category 1. Most business deductions, such as advertising, utilities, and employee costs, would fall into this category.

Category 3: Any deductions that reduce the basis of property, such as depreciation or amortization, or casualty losses can be deducted, but only to the extent that the gross income from your activity is in excess of the deductions already taken in Category 1 and Category 2. If you are a sole proprietor, your Category 2 and Category 3 deductions would be listed as Miscellaneous Deductions on Schedule A. They cannot exceed 2% of your adjusted grow income.

For partnerships, corporations, and LLCs, they would be reported at the business level on the K-1 or corporate return) and then passed on to the individual partner, shareholder, or member proportionately.

If you have several activities going on, you may combine them so long as they are interrelated either organizationally or economically, or they are natural extensions of each other, or they are similar in nature. Or you could choose to report the activities separately. Just make sure you keep good records in case the IRS has questions.

SECTION 1031 EXCHANGES

One of the best ways to reduce or defer taxes is by trading, or exchanging properties, both real estate and equipment, using the provisions of IRS Section 1031. Any property used in a trade or business can be exchanged.

One of the first rules of doing a 1031 Exchange is to work with professionals who understand the process. That includes an accountant, attorney, and title company.

To qualify as a 1031 Exchange, you must exchange your property or item (the relinquished property) for like-kind property or item (replacement property). The definition of like-kind is very broad in terms of real estate. For instance, you can exchange a 4-family apartment building for an office complex, or several single-family homes that you intend to rent.

Personal property has to be exchanged for items in the same property classification, so you can't exchange a truck for a passenger car, only another truck. But you can exchange one piece of office equipment for another piece of office equipment (a copier for a new telephone system, for instance).

If all parties are known and are in agreement, you can conduct a simultaneous closing or exchange your property in one transaction. Otherwise, you are dealing with several non-flexible deadlines. Once you dispose of your relinquished property, you have 45 days to identity the replacement property you plan to acquire.

You must then complete the transaction of transferring the replacement property into your name within 180 days of the sale or disposal of your relinquished property.

In order for the exchange to be tax-free, there can be no actual exchange of money. Therefore, 1031 Exchanges require that all exchange proceeds by paid and distributed out of an escrow account held by an escrow agent known as a Qualified Intermediary. The Qualified Intermediary must be completely independent of any buyer or seller and neither party can have no access to the funds until the transactions are complete and the escrow agent makes the required distributions and disclosures.

There are many companies who specialize in handling these types of transactions, so it may be well worth your time to interview them and use these services if your accountant or attorney is unclear on the procedures.

To benefit from the tax-free exchange, the replacement property you buy must be of equal or greater value than the property you relinquished. If your new property is less valuable, you will be forced to pay capital gain on your profits.

Reverse Like-Kind Exchanges

There are occasions when you may find the replacement property, and for various reasons, need to close on the transaction before you dispose of your relinquished property. This situation is known as a Reverse Like-Kind Exchange. This is permitted so long as the following procedures are followed:

Title of the replacement property cannot be held by you, but must be vested in an Exchange Accommodator (much like the Qualified Intermediary in a 1031 regular exchange). An Exchange Accommodator, however, must provide this service as a business, not as an individual.

When the Exchange Accommodator acquires the property, it must be specifically for the intent of holding it for the transferor.

Within five days of the transfer, there must be a contract in writing between the Exchange Accommodator and transferor specifying that this property is intended for a future 1031 Exchange and must acknowledge that the Exchange Accommodator is responsible for any taxes due on the property while it is in the possession of the Exchange Accommodator. However, the transferor may indemnify the Exchange Accommodator for costs and expenses incurred.

The property to be relinquished in exchange for the property being held must be identified within 45 days of property being transferred to the Exchange Accommodator.

Within 180 days of the transfer of the property to the Exchange Accommodator, the transaction transferring the property to the transferor must be completed.

CONCLUSION

The two most important keys to successfully minimizing your tax liability are: 1) Know the Rules (which you are well on your way to learning since you have read this book). But keep in mind, the tax rules change almost every year, so stay educated and seek help if you need it; and 2) Keep good records. Document everything. Maybe it's not a tax deduction, but at least put yourself through the exercise of thinking about each purchase to see if it CAN be deducted.

If you can actively think about the tax ramifications of your actions, you will find ways to keep more money in your pocket.

Happy deducting!

ABOUT THE AUTHOR

After being told in her early 30s that she had reached the pinnacle of her career in marketing, Katryna Johnson (known to her friends as Trina) knew she had to look for another challenge. She decided to enroll in law school, attending classes in the evenings and continuing to work fulltime during the day. Through a family crisis and unsteady corporate environment, she graduated with honors and passed the bar with ease. Using the marketing and business know-how learned from the corporate world, she took the entrepreneurship route and start her own firm instead of working for someone else.

In looking at the financial situation of a small business owner on the verge of bankruptcy, she discovered that he needed help and education about taxes and how to run his business, not bankruptcy. She began holding seminars to teach small business fundamentals to her clients.

After 10 years of divorces and bankruptcies and estates and small business litigation, she had discovered her true passion of helping others start-up and run small businesses. She formed Success Point Consulting, specializing in helping people (especially women) follow their dreams to start their own businesses. Through seminars and webinars, books, and one-on-one coaching and mentoring, she has been able to help hundreds of small business owners get on the path to success. She is especially passionate about helping small business owners establish a significant, vibrant online presence on websites, blogs, and through online social media.

With over 25 years of business management, marketing, and legal experience, she is a much sought-after speaker, presenter, and teacher on a wide range of business and motivational topics.